The CHICKEN or the EGG

Written & Illustrated by Bonnie Lemaire

The chicken or the egg
Copyright© 2017 Bonnie Lemaire
Published by Crowquill Publishing 2021

ISBN: 978-1-7771152-5-8 (paperback)
ISBN: 978-1-7771152-6-5 (hardcover)

Written by Bonnie Lemaire
Illustrations & cover by Bonnie Lemaire
Edited by Wanda Sloan

Summary :
Cornelia the Hen is stumped by a thought. Is it the chicken that comes first? Or is it the egg?
See who she encounters on her quest as she unwarily out smarts those she meets.
But even with her trickery will she make it back to her coop or become feathered treats!

Dedicated to all those in our feathered flock
who didn't escape Mr Fox .

Brenda, Mabel, Farrah and Faucet, and Vindaloo

Author Note: The names of the characters in this book have been changed to protect their identity.

Cornelia the Hen,
was usually smart as a fox,
but today, just today
she was stumped by a thought.

She went out for stroll,
flew the coop, one might say.
She pondered and wondered,
and wandered away....

She even stood on her head,
to think upside down!
She scratched and she pecked,
all with a discombobulated frown.

Out loud she went "Cluck- cluck",
and practically begged.
"What is it? What is it?
The chicken first or the egg?"

With that, Mr. Opossum waddled
out of the shade.
Mr. Opossum said *"he* had the answer."
and would exchange for a trade.

"For one delicious, uuh umm,
I mean delightful egg,
I will give you the truth!" he said.
Then he promptly twirled on one leg.

Something for something,
it is the way of the farm.
But Cornelia didn't want *her* eggs
to come to any harm.

So she hatched up a plan,
right there on the spot.
She would bring him an egg all right,
she knew the exact one to be got!

The farmer's kids had been playing,
and painted up some stones.
Bright colours for Easter
and hard as old bones.

She collected a few,
then returned on her quest.
Mr. Opossum was there waiting
in his very best dinner vest.

She tossed him her *egg* and cackled,
"lets have the truth!"
He hissed and he laughed and
chomped down breaking his tooth!

"The fox has your answer"
he groaned and he moaned.
He could't believe *he'd* been fooled
with one painted stone!

She hopped and she cackled,
and then took off in a hurry.
She still needed to know,
her mind was a flurry!

"What is it ? What is it?
What is it that comes first?
The chicken or the egg?"
Cornelia was about to burst!

Suddenly, she heard a
sweet sound by the bog,
Was it a lone mourning dove
or a sunbathing frog?

But to her horror, the low
"hoooot-hooot" turned to a growl,
and from behind the tree
flew a Great Horned Owl!

"Kuh-kuh-kuh-kuh-KACK!"

Cornelia gulped and let out a screech!
"Mr. Owl! Mr. Owl! please reconsider!
I could make you a bargain, a deal we could reach"
She DID NOT want to be Mr. Owl's DINNER!

Mr. Owl landed with a soft thump,
and two shakes of his leg,
then Cornelia timidly offered him
her special "rare egg".

He was very wise
and certainly no fool,
but to taste such a rare egg,
he would have to keep his cool.

I will let you go then
and even help you on your quest,
For I only know of one,
who would know best.

For such a mystery, such a quandary,
for this particular paradox,
You must go bravely, travel west,
and meet with Mr. Fox.

With that she turned swiftly
and scuffled off with a hop.
For an answer to her conundrum,
she had only one last *egg* to swap.

Down the path then round a corner
by Farmer Jim's old Cattle Ranch,
She spotted Mr. Fox,
just behind a bramble branch.

Mr Fox, stretched
and let out an exagerated yawn.
He had heard of this hen and her tricks
from a farm far beyond.

He would outsmart her he thought.
She was easy pick'ens.
She would be the most delightful,
the most delicious chicken of all chickens!

Cornelia stood tall,
knees quivering just a bit.
She said "Hello Mr. Fox,
I've traveled very far
in pursuit of your wit."

"A curious dilemma
I have found myself in,
I am in search of an answer to a question
that has gotten under my skin!"

"Oh what is it? What is it?
clearly you must know.
Is it first the chicken or the egg?
The chicken? yes or no!"

Aaaah thought Mr Fox,
putting his paw on his chin.
"This is quite a pickle
you've gotten yourself in."

"But to be honest, it doesn't really matter,
my new feathered friend.
They both taste the same,
the egg and the hen!"

With that Cornelia gasped
and let out a cackled cry!
Mr. Fox pounced from the bush
as he was really quite spry!

Cornelia just then pulled out
her last *egg* shaped rock!
And tossed it as hard as she could
with a terrified "squawk!"

It hit him on target
square in the nose!

Sending Mr. Fox flying head over toes!

She just barely escaped
with all her feathers intact.
Safe back in her coop
she is now resigned to the fact,

Whether the chicken came first,
or the egg, it didn't really matter,
The debate in itself
makes for fun chicken chitter chatter.

The End!

A few Feathery Fowl Facts!

Did you know that chickens have prehistoric roots and are the closest living relative of the Tyrannosaurus Rex!

Chickens have their own unique language with over 30 different sounds that they use to communicate. A few in this book are:

"Cluck Cluck" is the sound they make when they are wondering and starting their day.

"Kuh-kuh-kuh-kuh-KACK" is the sound of alarm!

"Cackle Cackle" - is the sound of general busy-ness or a sence of annoyance.

If chickens listen to classical music, they can lay bigger and heavier eggs.

In order to clean themselves, chickens take dust baths. They dig a small pit in the ground and use the dirt to help with the oil in their feathers.

Chickens can run up to 9 miles per hour! They love to play and will run, jump and sunbathe when given the chance.

Chickens have three eyelids. and can see in full colour just like we do. They will even respond to bright colors such as orange, red, green, and sometimes the colour blue is preferred by chickens. They can even recognise their human friends! So wear your favorite bright sweater when you visit the coop!

But chickens do not have night vision, so they cannot see in the dark. make sure they are all tucked in their coop at night!

And last and most suprising chickens can even burp and fart like you!

CPSIA information can be obtained
at www.ICGtesting.com
Printed in the USA
BVHW021752200721
612416BV00007B/1094